The Delicious Vegan Keto Cooking Guide

A Recipe Collection to Improve your Vegan Diet

Karen Yosco

Table of Contents

BREAKFAST

Chocolate Chip Coconut Pancakes

Preparation Time: 5 minutes

Cooking Time: 30 minutes

Servings: 8 servings

Ingredients:

- 11/4 cup oats

- 2 teaspoons coconut flakes

- 2 cup plant milk

- 11/4 cup maple syrup

- 11/3 cup of chocolate chips

- 2 1/4 cups buckwheat flour

- 2 teaspoon baking powder

- 1 teaspoon vanilla essence

- 2 teaspoon flaxseed meal

- Salt (optional)

Directions:

1. Put the flaxseed and cook over medium heat until the paste becomes a little moist.

2. Remove seeds.

3. Stir the buckwheat, oats, coconut chips, baking powder and salt with each other in a wide dish.

4. In a large dish, stir together the retained flax water with the sugar, maple syrup, vanilla essence.

5. Transfer the wet mixture to the dry **Ingredients:** and shake to combine

6. Place over medium heat the nonstick grill pan.

7. Pour 1/4 cup flour onto the grill pan with each pancake, and scatter gently.

8. Cook for five to six minutes, before the pancakes appear somewhat crispy.

Nutrition: Calories: 198 Fat: 9.1g Carbohydrates: 11.5g Protein: 7.9g

Apple-Lemon Bowl

Preparation Time: 5 minutes

Cooking Time: 15 minutes

Servings: 1-2 servings

Ingredients:

- 6 apples

- 3 tablespoons walnuts

- 7 dates

- Lemon juice

- 1/2 teaspoon cinnamon

Directions:

1. Root the apples, then break them into wide bits.

2. In a food cup, put seeds, part of the lime juice, almonds, spices and three-quarters of the apples. Thinly slice until finely ground.

3. Apply the remaining apples and lemon juice and make slices.

Nutrition: Calories: 249 Fat: 5.1g Carbohydrates: 71.5g Protein: 7.9g

Breakfast Scramble

Preparation Time: 10 minutes

Cooking Time: 30 minutes

Servings: 6 servings

Ingredients:

- 1 red onion1 to

- 2 tablespoons soy sauce

- 2 cups sliced mushrooms

- Salt to taste

- 11/2 teaspoon black pepper

- 11/2 teaspoons turmeric

- 1/4 teaspoon cayenne

- 3 cloves garlic

- 1 red bell pepper

- 1 large head cauliflower

- 1 green bell pepper

Directions:

1. In a small pan, put all vegetables and cook until crispy.

2. Stir in the cauliflower and cook for four to six minutes or until it smooth.

3. Add spices to the pan and cook for another five minutes.

Nutrition: Calories: 199 Fat: 1.1g Carbohydrates: 14.5g Protein: 7.9g

LUNCH

Green Bean Casserole

Preparation Time: 5 minutes

Cooking Time: 40 minutes

Servings: 4

Ingredients:

- 6 ounces fried onions

- 1 ½ cups cremini mushrooms, diced

- 16 ounces frozen green beans

- ½ cup diced white onion

- 1 tablespoon minced garlic

- 3 ½ tablespoons all-purpose flour

- 1/3 teaspoon ground black pepper

- ½ teaspoon dried oregano

- 3 ½ tablespoons olive oil

- 2 cups vegetable broth, hot

Directions:

1. Switch on the oven, then set it to 400 degrees F and let it preheat.

2. Take a medium saucepan, place it over medium heat, add oil and when hot, add onion and mushrooms, stir in garlic and cook for 4 minutes until tender.

3. Stir in flour until the thick paste comes together and then cook for 2 minutes until golden.

4. Stir in vegetable broth, bring it to a simmer, then stir in black pepper and oregano, whisk well and cook for 15 minutes until gravy thickened to the desired level.

5. Add green beans, stir until mixed, remove the pan from heat, top beans with fried onions and bake for 15 minutes.

6. Serve straight away.

Nutrition: 191 Cal 10 g Fat 2 g Saturated Fat 22 g Carbohydrates 3.3 g Fiber 2.5 g Sugars 4.1 g Protein;

Pumpkin Risotto

Preparation Time: 5 minutes

Cooking Time: 20 minutes

Servings: 4

Ingredients:

- 1 cup Arborio rice

- ½ cup cooked and chopped pumpkin

- 1/2 cup mushrooms

- 1 rib of celery, diced

- ½ of a medium white onion, peeled, diced

- ½ teaspoon minced garlic

- ½ teaspoon salt

- 1/3 teaspoon ground black pepper

- 1 tablespoon olive oil

- ½ tablespoon coconut butter

- 1 cup pumpkin puree

- 2 cups vegetable stock

Directions:

1. Take a medium saucepan, place it over medium heat, add oil and when hot, add onion and celery, stir in garlic and cook for 3 minutes until onions begin to soften.

2. Add mushrooms, season with salt and black pepper and cook for 5 minutes.

3. Add rice, pour in pumpkin puree, then gradually pour in the stock until rice soaked up all the liquid and have turned soft.

4. Add butter, remove the pan from heat, stir until creamy mixture comes together, and then serve.

Nutrition: 218.5 Cal 5.2 g Fat 1.5 g Saturated Fat 32.3 g Carbohydrates 1.3 g Fiber 3.8 g Sugars 6.3 g Protein;

Tomato Basil Spaghetti

Preparation Time: 5 minutes

Cooking Time: 20 minutes

Servings: 4

Ingredients:

- 15-ounce cooked great northern beans

- 10.5-ounces cherry tomatoes, halved

- 1 small white onion, peeled, diced

- 1 tablespoon minced garlic

- 8 basil leaves, chopped

- 2 tablespoons olive oil

- 1-pound spaghetti

Directions:

1. Take a large pot half full with salty water, place it over medium-high heat, bring it to a boil, add spaghetti and cook for 10 to 12 minutes until tender.

2. Then drain spaghetti into a colander and reserve 1 cup of pasta liquid.

3. Take a large skillet pan, place it over medium-high heat, add oil and when hot, add onion, tomatoes, basil, and garlic and cook for 5 minutes until vegetables have turned tender.

4. Add cooked spaghetti and beans, pour in pasta water, stir until just mixed and cook for 2 minutes until hot.

5. Serve straight away.

Nutrition: 147 Cal 5 g Fat 0.7 g Saturated Fat 21.2 g Carbohydrates 1.5 g Fiber 5.4 g Sugars 3.8 g Protein

DINNER

Black Bean Burgers

Preparation Time: 10 minutes

Cooking Time: 15 minutes

Servings: 6

Ingredients:

- 1 Onion, diced

- ½ cup Corn Nibs

- 2 Cloves Garlic, minced

- ½ teaspoon Oregano, dried

- ½ cup Flour

- 1 Jalapeno Pepper, small

- 2 cups Black Beans, mashed & canned

- ¼ cup Breadcrumbs (Vegan)

- 2 teaspoons Parsley, minced

- ¼ teaspoon cumin

- 1 tablespoon Olive Oil

- 2 teaspoons Chili Powder

- ½ Red Pepper, diced

- Sea Salt to taste

Directions:

1. Set your flour on a plate, and then get out your garlic, onion, peppers and oregano, throwing it in a pan. Cook over medium-high heat, and then cook until the onions are translucent. Place the peppers in, and sauté until tender.

2. Cook for two minutes, and then set it to the side.

3. Use a potato masher to mash your black beans, then stir in the vegetables, cumin, breadcrumbs, parsley, salt, and chili powder, and then divide it into six patties.

4. Coat each side, and then cook until it is fried on each side.

Nutrition: Calories: 357 kcal Protein: 17.93 g Fat: 5.14 g Carbohydrates: 61.64 g

Dijon Maple Burgers

Preparation Time: 20 minutes

Cooking Time: 30 minutes

Servings: 12

Ingredients:

- 1 Red Bell Pepper

- 19 ounces Can Chickpeas, rinsed & drained

- 1 cup Almonds, ground

- 2 teaspoons Dijon Mustard

- 1 teaspoon Oregano

- ½ teaspoon Sage

- 1 cup Spinach, fresh

- 1 – ½ cups Rolled Oats

- 1 Clove Garlic, pressed

- ½ Lemon, juiced

- 2 teaspoons Maple Syrup, pure

Directions:

1. Get out a baking sheet. Line it with parchment paper.

2. Cut your red pepper in half and then take the seeds out. Place it on your baking sheet, and roast in the oven while you prepare your other ingredients.

3. Process your chickpeas, almonds, mustard, and maple syrup together in a food processor.

4. Add in your lemon juice, oregano, sage, garlic, and spinach, processing again. Make sure it's combined, but don't puree it.

5. Once your red bell pepper is softened, which should roughly take ten minutes, add this to the processor as well. Add in your oats, mixing well.

6. Form twelve patties, cooking in the oven for a half-hour. They should be browned.

Nutrition: Calories: 96 kcal Protein: 5.28 g Fat: 2.42 g Carbohydrates: 16.82 g

Hearty Black Lentil Curry

Preparation Time: 30 minutes

Cooking Time: 6 hours and 15 minutes

Servings: 4

Ingredients:

- 1 cup of black lentils, rinsed and soaked overnight

- 14 ounce of chopped tomatoes

- 2 large white onions, peeled and sliced

- 1 1/2 teaspoon of minced garlic

- 1 teaspoon of grated ginger

- 1 red chili

- 1 teaspoon of salt

- 1/4 teaspoon of red chili powder

- 1 teaspoon of paprika

- 1 teaspoon of ground turmeric

- 2 teaspoons of ground cumin

- 2 teaspoons of ground coriander

- 1/2 cup of chopped coriander

- 4-ounce of vegetarian butter

- 4 fluid of ounce water

- 2 fluid of ounce vegetarian double cream

Directions:

1. Place a large pan over moderate heat, add butter and let heat until melt.

2. Add the onion and garlic and ginger and cook for 10 to 15 minutes or until onions are caramelized.

3. Then stir in salt, red chili powder, paprika, turmeric, cumin, ground coriander, and water.

4. Transfer this mixture to a 6-quarts slow cooker and add tomatoes and red chili.

5. Drain lentils, add to slow cooker, and stir until just mix.

6. Plugin slow cooker; adjust cooking time to 6 hours and let cook on low heat setting.

7. When the lentils are done, stir in cream and adjust the seasoning.

8. Serve with boiled rice or whole wheat bread.

Nutrition: Calories: 299 kcal Protein: 5.59 g Fat: 27.92 g Carbohydrates: 9.83 g

Flavorful Refried Beans

Preparation Time: 15 minutes

Cooking Time: 8 hours

Servings: 8

Ingredients:

- 3 cups of pinto beans, rinsed

- 1 small jalapeno pepper, seeded and chopped

- 1 medium-sized white onion, peeled and sliced

- 2 tablespoons of minced garlic

- 5 teaspoons of salt

- 2 teaspoons of ground black pepper

- 1/4 teaspoon of ground cumin

- 9 cups of water

Directions:

1. Using a 6-quarts slow cooker, place all the ingredients and stir until it mixes properly.

2. Cover the top, plug in the slow cooker, adjust the cooking time to 6 hours, let it cook on the high heat setting, and add more water if the beans get too dry.

3. When the beans are done, drain it then reserve the liquid.

4. Mash the beans using a potato masher and pour in the reserved cooking liquid until it reaches your desired mixture.

5. Serve immediately.

Nutrition: Calories: 268 kcal Protein: 16.55 g Fat: 1.7 g Carbohydrates: 46.68 g

STIR-FRIED, GRILLED VEGETABLES

Grilled Portobello

Preparation Time: 10 minutes

Cooking Time: 8 minutes

Servings: 04

Ingredients:

- 4 portobello mushrooms
- ¼ cup soy sauce
- ¼ cup tomato sauce
- 2 tablespoons maple syrup
- 1 tablespoon molasses
- 2 tablespoons minced garlic
- 1 tablespoon onion powder
- 1 pinch salt and pepper

Directions:

1. Mix all the ingredients except mushrooms in a bowl.
2. Add mushrooms to this marinade and mix well to coat.
3. Cover and marinate for 1 hour.
4. Prepare and set up the grill at medium heat. Grease it with cooking spray.
5. Grill the mushroom for 4 minutes per side.
6. Serve

Nutrition: Calories: 404 Total Fat: 43g Carbs: 8g Net Carbs: 4g Fiber: 1g Protein: 4g

Wok Fried Broccoli

Preparation Time: 10 minutes

Cooking Time: 16 minutes

Servings: 02

Ingredients:

- 3 ounces whole, blanched peanuts

- 2 tablespoons olive oil

- 1 banana shallot, sliced

- 10 ounces broccoli, trimmed and cut into florets

- ¼ red pepper, julienned

- ½ yellow pepper, julienned

- 1 teaspoon soy sauce

Directions:

1. Toast peanuts on a baking sheet for 15 minutes at 350 degrees F.

2. In a wok, add oil and shallots and sauté for 10 minutes.

3. Toss in broccoli and peppers.

4. Stir fry for 3 minutes then add the rest of the ingredients.

5. Cook for 3 additional minutes and serve.

Nutrition: Calories: 391 Total Fat: 39g Carbs: 15g Net Carbs: 5g Fiber: 2g Protein: 6g

DIP AND SPREAD RECIPES

Maple Bagel Spread

Preparation Time: 10 minutes

Cooking Time: 10 minutes

Servings: 1

Ingredients:

- cream cheese

- maple syrup

- cinnamon

- walnuts

Directions:

1. Beat the cinnamon, syrup, and cream cheese in a big bowl until it becomes smooth, then mix in walnuts.

2. Let it chill until ready to serve. Serve it with bagels.

Nutrition: Calories 586 Fat 7 Carbs 23 Protein 4

Italian Stuffed Artichokes

Preparation Time: 20 minutes

Cooking Time: 25 minutes

Servings: 4

Ingredients:

- 4 large artichokes

- 2 teaspoon lemon juice

- 2 cups soft Italian bread crumbs, toasted

- 1/2 cup grated Parmigiano-Reggiano cheese

- 1/2 cup minced fresh parsley

- 2 teaspoon Italian seasoning

- 1 teaspoon grated lemon peel

- 1/2 teaspoon pepper

- 1/4 teaspoon salt

- 1 tablespoon olive oil

Directions:

1. Level the bottom of each artichoke using a sharp knife and trim off 1-inch from the tops. Snip off tips of outer leaves

using kitchen scissors, then brush lemon juice on cut edges. In a Dutch oven, stand the artichokes and pour 1-inch of water, then boil. Lower the heat, put the cover, and let it simmer for 5 minutes or until the leaves near the middle pull out effortlessly.

2. Turn the artichokes upside down to drain. Allow it to stand for 10 minutes. Carefully scrape out the fuzzy middle part of the artichokes using a spoon and get rid of it.

3. Mix the salt, pepper, lemon peel, Italian seasoning, garlic, parsley, cheese, and breadcrumbs in a small bowl, then add olive oil and stir well. Gently spread the artichoke leaves apart, then fill it with breadcrumb mixture.

4. Put it in a cooking spray-coated 11x7-inch baking dish. Let it bake for 10 minutes at 350 degrees F without cover, or until the filling turns light brown.

Nutrition: Calories 543 Fat 5 Carbs 44 Protein 6

PASTA & NOODLES

Creamy Vegan Spinach Pasta

Preparation Time: 20 minutes

Cooking Time: 5 minutes

Servings: 4

Ingredients:

- 1 cup raw cashews, soaked in water for 8 hours

- 2 tablespoons lemon juice

- 1 tablespoon olive oil

- 1½ cups vegetable broth

- 2 tablespoons fresh dill, chopped

- Red pepper flakes, to taste

- 10 ounces dried fusilli

- ½ cup almond milk, unflavored and unsweetened

- 2 tablespoons white miso paste

- 4 garlic cloves, divided

- 8-ounces fresh spinach, finely chopped

- ¼ cup scallions, chopped

- Salt and black pepper, to taste

Directions:

1. Boil salted water in a large pot and add pasta.

2. Cook according to the package directions and drain the pasta into a colander.

3. Dish out the pasta in a large serving bowl and add a dash of olive oil to prevent sticking.

4. Put the cashews, milk, miso, lemon juice, and 1 garlic clove into the food processor and blend until smooth.

5. Put olive oil over medium heat in a large pot and add the remaining 3 cloves of garlic.

6. Sauté for about 1 minute and stir in the spinach and broth.

7. Raise the heat and allow to simmer for about 4 minutes until the spinach is bright green and wilted.

8. Stir in the pasta and cashew mixture and season with salt and black pepper.

9. Top with scallions and dill and dish out into plates to serve.

Nutrition: Calories: 94 Total Fat: 10g Protein: 0g Total Carbs: 1g Fiber: 0.3g Net Carbs: 0.7g

SIDE DISHES

Three-Lentil Curry

Preparation Time: 10 min

Cooking Time: 25 min

Servings: 2

Ingredients:

- ½ tablespoon coconut oil

- 1 teaspoon garlic powder

- 1 teaspoon ginger powder

- ½ tablespoon garam masala

- 1 teaspoon cumin powder

- ¼ teaspoon turmeric powder

- ¼ teaspoon table salt

- ¼ teaspoon paprika

- 1 cinnamon stick 4-inch stick

- 2 green cardamom pods

- 1 bay leave

- ½ cup red tomatoes chopped

- ¼ cup red lentils

- ¼ cup brown lentils

- ¼ cup green lentils

- ¼ cup

- 4 cups water

- 1/2 cup coconut cream

Directions:

1. Press Sauté, set time for 5 minutes.

2. Add coconut oil in the Instant Pot. Add the garlic powder, ginger powder, garam masala, cumin powder, turmeric powder, salt, paprika, cinnamon stick, cardamom pods, and bay leaves. Stir until fragrant, about 1 minute. Add the tomatoes and cook, stirring often, until it just begins to break down, 1 to 2 minutes.

3. Turn off the Sauté function. Stir in the red lentils, brown lentils, and green lentils until coated in the spices. Stir in the water and lock the lid onto the Instant Pot.

4. Press Pressure Cook on Max Pressure for 16 minutes with the Keep Warm setting off.

5. Use the Quick-release method to bring the Instant Pot pressure back to normal. Unlatch the lid and open the Instant pot. Remove and discard the cinnamon stick, cardamom pods, and bay leaves. Stir in the cream until uniform, then set the lid askew over the Instant Pot for 5 minutes to blend the flavors. Stir again before serving.

Nutrition: Calories 340, Total Fat 21. 1g, Saturated Fat 16. 3g, Cholesterol 0mg, Sodium 390mg, Total Carbohydrate 30. 8g, Dietary Fiber 10. 8g, Total Sugars 5. 7g, Protein 10. 4g

Chickpea Curry

Preparation Time: 10 min

Cooking Time: 30 min

Servings: 2

Ingredients:

- ½ cup dried chickpeas rinsed
- 2 cups water
- 1 tablespoon vegetable oil
- ½ teaspoon cumin seeds
- 1 small onion finely diced
- ½ teaspoon ginger powder
- ½ teaspoon garlic powder
- ½ tablespoon coriander powder
- 1 teaspoon salt
- ¼ teaspoon turmeric powder
- 1 tomatoes cored and finely diced,
- ½ cup parsley fresh, chopped
- 1/4 teaspoon garam masala

Directions:

1. In a bowl, combine the chickpeas and 2 cups warm water and let soak for at least 4 hours or up to overnight. Drain the chickpeas and set aside.

2. Select the High Sauté setting on the Instant Pot and heat the vegetable oil. Add the cumin seeds directly to the hot oil at the bottom edges of the Instant Pot and cook until they start to sizzle, about 1 minute. Add the chopped onions and cook, stirring occasionally, until translucent, about 5 minutes. Add the ginger powder and garlic powder and sauté until aromatic, about 1 minute. Add the coriander powder, salt, turmeric powder, and chickpeas; pour in the 2 cups water; and stir well.

3. Secure the lid and set the Pressure Release to Sealing. Press the Cancel button to reset the cooking program, then select the Pressure Cook or Manual setting and set the cooking time for 35 minutes at High Pressure.

4. Let the pressure release naturally; this will take 10 to 20 minutes. Open the pot and stir in the tomatoes and garam masala. Select the High Sauté setting and cook until the tomatoes soften, about 5 minutes. Press the Cancel button to turn off the Instant Pot. Ladle into bowls, sprinkle with the parsley, and serve.

Nutrition: Calories 202, Total Fat 9. 2g, Saturated Fat 1. 4g, Cholesterol 0mg, Sodium 1186mg, Total Carbohydrate 27. 9g, Dietary Fiber 7. 8g, Total Sugars 7. 3g, Protein 8. 2g

Pumpkin Stew

Preparation Time: 10 min

Cooking Time: 15 min

Servings: 2

Ingredients:

- 1 cup vegetable broth

- 1 1/2 cups pumpkin cut into small cubes

- 1 cup kidney beans cooked, rinsed and drained

- 1 cup onion chopped

- ½ cup green peas

- 1 teaspoon garlic powder

- ½ cup diced tomatoes

- 1 teaspoon red chili

- ¼ teaspoon ground cumin

Directions:

1. Place all the ingredients in the inner pot. Cover with lid, turn lid clockwise to lock into place. Align the pointed end of the steam release handle to point to "Sealing". Press

"Manual", use [-] button to adjust cooking time to 5 minutes.

2. When cooking time is complete, press "Keep Warm/Cancel" once to Cancel the keep warm mode then wait 10 minutes for the pressure to go down.

3. Slide the steam release handle to the "Venting" position to release remaining pressure until the float valve drops down.

4. Remove lid. Allow to cool 10 minutes before serving. Enjoy!

Nutrition: Calories245, Total Fat 2. 4g, Saturated Fat 0. 4g, Cholesterol 0mg, Sodium 805mg, Total Carbohydrate 43. 2g, Dietary Fiber 13. 6g, Total Sugars 11. 4g, Protein 14. 5g

SOUP AND STEW

Coconut and Grilled Vegetable Soup

Preparation Time: 10 Minutes

Cooking Time: 45 Minutes

Servings: 4

Ingredients:

- 2 small red onions cut into wedges

- 2 garlic cloves

- 10 oz. butternut squash, peeled and chopped

- 10 oz. pumpkins, peeled and chopped

- 4 tbsp. melted vegan butter

- Salt and black pepper to taste

- 1 cup of water

- 1 cup unsweetened coconut milk

- 1 lime juiced

- ¾ cup vegan mayonnaise

- Toasted pumpkin seeds for garnishing

Directions:

1. Preheat the oven to 400 F.

2. On a baking sheet, spread the onions, garlic, butternut squash, and pumpkins and drizzle half of the butter on top. Season with salt, black pepper, and rub the seasoning well onto the vegetables. Roast in the oven for 45 minutes or until the vegetables are golden brown and softened.

3. Transfer the vegetables to a pot; add the remaining ingredients except for the pumpkin seeds and using an immersion blender puree the ingredients until smooth.

4. Dish the soup, garnish with the pumpkin seeds and serve warm.

Nutrition: Calories 290 Fat 10 g Protein 30 g Carbohydrates 0 g

Broccoli Fennel Soup

Preparation Time: 15 Minutes

Cooking Time: 10 Minutes

Servings: 4

Ingredients:

- 1 fennel bulb, white and green parts coarsely chopped

- 10 oz. broccoli, cut into florets

- 3 cups vegetable stock

- Salt and freshly ground black pepper

- 1 garlic clove

- 1 cup dairy-free cream cheese

- 3 oz. vegan butter

- ½ cup chopped fresh oregano

Directions:

1. In a medium pot, combine the fennel, broccoli, vegetable stock, salt, and black pepper. Bring to a boil until the vegetables soften, 10 to 15 minutes.

2. Stir in the remaining ingredients and simmer the soup for 3 to 5 minutes.

3. Adjust the taste with salt and black pepper, and dish the soup.

4. Serve warm.

Nutrition: Calories 240 Fat 0 g Protein 0 g Carbohydrates 20 g

Tofu Goulash Soup

Preparation Time: 35 Minutes

Cooking Time: 20 Minutes

Servings: 4

Ingredients:

- 4¼ oz. vegan butter

- 1 white onion, chopped

- 2 garlic cloves, minced

- 1 ½ cups butternut squash

- 1 red bell pepper, deseeded and chopped

- 1 tbsp. paprika powder

- ¼ tsp red chili flakes

- 1 tbsp. dried basil

- ½ tbsp. crushed cardamom seeds

- Salt and black pepper to taste

- 1 ½ cups crushed tomatoes

- 3 cups vegetable broth

- 1½ tsp red wine vinegar

- Chopped parsley to serve

Directions:

1. Place the tofu between two paper towels and allow draining of water for 30 minutes. After, crumble the tofu and set aside.

2. Melt the vegan butter in a large pot over medium heat and sauté the onion and garlic until the veggies are fragrant and soft, 3 minutes.

3. Stir in the tofu and cook until golden brown, 3 minutes.

4. Add the butternut squash, bell pepper, paprika, red chili flakes, basil, cardamom seeds, salt, and black pepper. Cook for 2 minutes to release some flavor and mix in the tomatoes and 2 cups of vegetable broth.

5. Close the lid, bring the soup to a boil, and then simmer for 10 minutes.

6. Stir in the remaining vegetable broth, the red wine vinegar, and adjust the taste with salt and black pepper.

7. Dish the soup, garnish with the parsley and serve warm.

Nutrition: Calories 320 Fat 10 g Protein 10 g Carbohydrates 20 g

Pesto Pea Soup

Preparation Time: 10 Minutes

Cooking Time: 20 Minutes

Servings: 4

Ingredients:

- 2 cups Water

- 8 oz. Tortellini

- ¼ cup Pesto

- 1 Onion, small & finely chopped

- 1 lb. Peas, frozen

- 1 Carrot, medium & finely chopped

- 1 ¾ cup Vegetable Broth, less sodium

- 1 Celery Rib, medium & finely chopped

Directions:

1. To start with, boil the water in a large pot over a medium-high heat.

2. Next, stir in the tortellini to the pot and cook it following the instructions given in the packet.

3. In the meantime, cook the onion, celery, and carrot in a deep saucepan along with the water and broth.

4. Cook the celery-onion mixture for 6 minutes or until softened.

5. Now, spoon in the peas and allow it to simmer while keeping it uncovered.

6. Cook the peas for few minutes or until they are bright green and soft.

7. Then, spoon in the pesto to the peas mixture. Combine well.

8. Pour the mixture into a high-speed blender and blend for 2 to 3 minutes or until you get a rich, smooth soup.

9. Return the soup to the pan. Spoon in the cooked tortellini.

10. Finally, pour into a serving bowl and top with more cooked peas if desired.

11. Tip: If desired, you can season it with Maldon salt at the end.

Nutrition: Calories 100 Fat 0 g Protein 0 g Carbohydrates 0 g

Avocado Green Soup

Preparation Time: 5 Minutes

Cooking Time: 5 Minutes

Servings: 4

Ingredients:

- 2 tbsp. olive oil

- 1 ½ cup fresh kale, chopped coarsely

- 1 ½ cup fresh spinach, chopped coarsely

- 3 large avocados, halved, pitted and pulp extracted

- 2 cups of soy milk

- 2 cups no-sodium vegetable broth

- 3 tbsp. chopped fresh mint leaves

- ¼ tsp salt

- ¼ tsp black pepper

- 2 limes, juiced

Directions:

1. Heat the olive oil in a medium saucepan over medium heat and mix in the kale and spinach. Cook until wilted, 3 minutes and turn off the heat.

2. Add the remaining ingredients and using an immersion blender, puree the soup until smooth.

3. Dish the soup and serve immediately.

Nutrition: Calories 400 Fat 10 g Protein 20 g Carbohydrates 30 g

Black Bean Nacho Soup

Preparation Time: 5 Minutes

Cooking Time: 30 Minutes

Servings: 4

Ingredients:

- 30 oz. Black Bean

- 1 tbsp. Olive Oil

- 2 cups Vegetable Stock

- ½ of 1 Onion, large & chopped

- 2 ½ cups Water

- 3 Garlic cloves, minced

- 14 oz. Mild Green Chillies, diced

- 1 tsp. Cumin

- 1 cup Salsa

- ½ tsp. Salt

- 16 oz. Tomato Paste

- ½ tsp. Black Pepper

Directions:

1. For making this delicious fare, heat oil in a large pot over medium-high heat.

2. Once the oil becomes hot, stir in onion and garlic to it.

3. Sauté for 4 minutes or until the onion is softened.

4. Next, spoon in chili powder, salt, cumin, and pepper to the pot. Mix well.

5. Then, stir in tomato paste, salsa, water, green chillies, and vegetable stock to onion mixture. Combine.

6. Bing the mixture to a boil. Allow the veggies to simmer.

7. When the mixture starts simmering, add the beans.

8. Bring the veggie mixture to a simmer again and lower the heat to low.

9. Finally, cook for 15 to 20 minutes and check for seasoning. Add more salt and pepper if needed.

10. Garnish with the topping of your choice. Serve it hot.

Nutrition: Calories 270 Fat 10 g Protein 10 g Carbohydrates 10 g

Potato Leek Soup

Preparation Time: 5 Minutes

Cooking Time: 5 Minutes

Servings: 4

Ingredients:

- 1 cup fresh cilantro leaves

- 6 garlic cloves, peeled

- 3 tbsp. vegetable oil

- 3 leeks, white and green parts chopped

- 2 lb. russet potatoes, peeled and chopped

- 1 tsp cumin powder

- ¼ tsp salt

- ¼ tsp black pepper

- 2 bay leaves

- 6 cups no-sodium vegetable broth

Directions:

1. In a spice blender, process the cilantro and garlic until smooth paste forms.

2. Heat the vegetable oil in a large pot and sauté the garlic mixture and leeks until the leeks are tender, 5 minutes.

3. Mix in the remaining ingredients and allow boiling until the potatoes soften, 15 minutes.

4. Turn the heat off, open the lid, remove and discard the bay leaves.

5. Using an immersion blender, puree the soup until smooth.

6. Dish the food and serve warm.

Nutrition: Calories 215 Fat 0 g Protein 10 g Carbohydrates 20.0 g

SMOOTHIES AND BEVERAGES

Beet and Clementine Protein Smoothie

Preparation Time: 10 minutes

Cooking Time: 0 minutes

Servings: 3

Ingredients:

- 1 small beet, peeled and chopped

- 1 clementine, peeled and broken into segments

- ½ ripe banana

- ½ cup raspberries

- 1 tablespoon chia seeds

- 2 tablespoons almond butter

- ¼ teaspoon vanilla extract

- 1 cup unsweetened almond milk

- 1/8 teaspoon fine sea salt, optional

Directions:

1. Combine all the ingredients in a food processor, then pulse on high for 2 minutes or until glossy and creamy.

2. Refrigerate for an hour and serve chilled.

Nutrition: Calories: 526 Fat: 25.4g Carbs: 61.9g Fiber: 17.3g Protein: 20.6g

BREAD RECIPES

Potato Bread

Preparation Time: 3 hours

Cooking Time: 45 minutes

Servings: 2 loaves

Ingredients:

- 1 3/4 teaspoon active dry yeast

- tablespoon dry milk

- 1/4 cup instant potato flakes

- tablespoon sugar

- cups bread flour

- 1 1/4 teaspoon salt

- tablespoon butter

- 1 3/8 cups water

Directions:

1 Put all the liquid ingredients in the pan. Add all the dry ingredients, except the yeast. Form a shallow hole in the middle of the dry ingredients and place the yeast.

2 Secure the pan in the machine and close the lid. Choose the basic setting and your desired color of the crust. Press starts.

3 Allow the bread to cool before slicing.

Nutrition: Calories: 35calories; Total Carbohydrate: 19 g Total Fat: 0 g Protein: 4 g

Onion Potato Bread

Preparation Time: 1 hour 20 minutes

Cooking Time: 45 minutes

Servings: 2 loaves

Ingredients:

- tablespoon quick rise yeast

- cups bread flour

- 1 1/2 teaspoon seasoned salt

- tablespoon sugar

- 2/3 cup baked potatoes, mashed

- 1 1/2 cup onions, minced

- large eggs

- tablespoon oil

- 3/4 cup hot water, with the temperature of 115 to 125 degrees F (46 to 51 degrees C)

Directions:

1 Put the liquid ingredients in the pan. Add the dry ingredients, except the yeast. Form a shallow well in the middle using your hand and put the yeast.

2 Place the pan in the machine, close the lid and turn it on. Select the express bake 80 setting and start the machine.

3 Once the bread is cooked, leave on a wire rack for 20 minutes or until cooled.

Nutrition: Calories: 160calories; Total Carbohydrate: 44 g Total Fat: 2 g Protein: 6 g

Spinach Bread

Preparation Time: 2 hours 20 minutes

Cooking Time: 40 minutes

Servings: 1 loaf

Ingredients:

- 1 cup water

- 1 tablespoon vegetable oil

- 1/2 cup frozen chopped spinach, thawed and drained

- cups all-purpose flour

- 1/2 cup shredded Cheddar cheese

- 1 teaspoon salt

- 1 tablespoon white sugar

- 1/2 teaspoon ground black pepper

- 1/2 teaspoons active dry yeast

Directions:

1 In the pan of bread machine, put all ingredients according to the suggested order of manufacture. Set white bread cycle.

Nutrition: Calories: 121 calories; Total Carbohydrate: 20.5 g Cholesterol: 4 mg Total Fat: 2.5 g Protein: 4 g

Sodium: 184 mg

SAUCES, DRESSINGS, AND DIPS

Easy Lemon Tahini Dressing

Preparation Time: 5 minutes

Cooking Time: 0 minutes

Servings: 1

Ingredients:

- ½ cup tahini

- ¼ cup fresh lemon juice (about 2 lemons)

- 1 teaspoon maple syrup

- 1 small garlic clove, chopped

- 1/8 teaspoon black pepper

- ¼ teaspoon salt (optional)

- ¼ to ½ cup water

Directions:

1. Process the tahini, lemon juice, maple syrup, garlic, black pepper, and salt (if desired) in a blender (high-speed blenders work best for this). Gradually add the water until the mixture is completely smooth.

2. Store in an airtight container in the fridge for up to 5 days.

Nutrition: Calories: 128 Fat: 9.6g Carbs: 6.8g Protein: 3.6g Fiber: 1.9g

SALADS RECIPES

Edamame & Ginger Citrus Salad

Preparation Time: 15 minutes

Cooking Time: 0 minutes

Servings: 3

Ingredients:

Dressing:

- ¼ cup orange juice

- 1 tsp. lime juice

- ½ tbsp. maple syrup

- ½ tsp. ginger, finely minced

- ½ tbsp. sesame oil

Salad:

- ½ cup dry green lentils

- 2 cups carrots, shredded

- 4 cups kale, fresh or frozen, chopped

- 1 cup edamame, shelled

- 1 tablespoon roasted sesame seeds

- 2 tsp. mint, chopped

- Salt and pepper to taste

- 1 small avocado, peeled, pitted, diced

Directions:

1. Prepare the lentils according to the method.

2. Combine the orange and lime juices, maple syrup, and ginger in a small bowl. Mix with a whisk while slowly adding the sesame oil.

3. Add the cooked lentils, carrots, kale, edamame, sesame seeds, and mint to a large bowl.

4. Add the dressing and stir well until all the ingredients are coated evenly.

5. Store or serve topped with avocado and an additional sprinkle of mint.

Nutrition: Calories 507 Total Fat 23.1g Saturated Fat 4g Cholesterol 0mg Sodium 303mg Total Carbohydrate 56.8g Dietary Fiber 21.6g Total Sugars 8.4g Protein 24.6g Vitamin D 0mcg Calcium 374mg Iron 8mg Potassium 1911mg

Chickpea and Spinach Salad

Preparation Time: 5 minutes

Cooking Time: 0 minutes

Servings: 4

Ingredients:

- 2 cans (14.5 ounces each) chickpeas, drained, rinsed

- 7 ounces vegan feta cheese, crumbled or chopped

- 1 tablespoon lemon juice

- 1/3 -½ cup olive oil

- ½ teaspoon salt or to taste

- 4-6 cups spinach, torn

- ½ cup raisins

- 2 tablespoons honey

- 1-2 teaspoons ground cumin

- 1 teaspoon chili flakes

Directions:

1. Add cheese, chickpeas and spinach into a large bowl.

2. To make dressing: Add rest of the ingredients into another bowl and mix well.

3. Pour dressing over the salad. Toss well and serve.

Nutrition: Calories 822 Total Fat 42.5g Saturated Fat 11.7g Cholesterol 44mg Sodium 910mg Total Carbohydrate 89.6g Dietary Fiber 19.7g Total Sugars 32.7g Protein 29g Vitamin D 0mcg Calcium 417mg Iron 9mg Potassium 1347mg

FRUIT SALAD RECIPES

Mimosa Salad

Preparation Time: 10 Minutes

Cooking Time: 0 Minutes

Servings: 8

Ingredients:

- Mint, fresh, one half cup

- Orange juice, one half cup

- Pineapple, one cup cut into small pieces

- Strawberries, one cup cut into quarters

- Blueberries, one cup

- Blackberries, one cup

- Kiwi, three peeled and sliced

Directions:

1. In a large-sized bowl, mix all of the fruits together and then top with the orange juice and the fresh mint.

2. Toss gently together all of the fruit until they are well mixed.

Nutrition: Calories: 215 Protein: 3g Fat: 1g Carbs: 49g

ENTRÉES

Italian "Meatball" Subs

Preparation Time: 5 minutes

Cooking Time: 55 minutes

Servings: 4

Ingredients:

- Chickpeas, liquid drained, rinsed – 15 ounces (1.5 cups)

- Bread crumbs - .25 cup

- Flaxseed, ground – 1.5 tablespoons

- Water, warm – .25 cup

- Nutritional yeast – 2 tablespoons

- Italian seasoning - .5 teaspoon

- Sea salt - .5 teaspoon

- Garlic powder – 2 teaspoons

- Sub rolls, medium – 3

- Vegan mozzarella cheese, shredded (such as Daiya or homemade) – .75 cup

- Marinara sauce – 1 cup

Directions:

1. Preheat your large oven to a temperature of Fahrenheit four-hundred and twenty-five degrees. Meanwhile, assemble your chickpea "meatballs."

2. In a medium-sized bowl for the purpose of mixing whisk together the warm water and flaxseed until all of the clumps are gone. Allow it to sit for five minutes.

3. Meanwhile, place the chickpeas in the food processor with the standard blade and pulse them until they are finely ground with no whole beans remaining. Place the chickpea meal into the bowl with the flaxseed mixture.

4. Add the sea salt, bread crumbs, Italian seasoning, nutritional yeast, and garlic powder to the chickpea and flaxseed bowl, combining the ingredients together completely with a spoon.

5. Using a mini cookie scoop or tablespoon measure out evenly sized "meatballs" with the mixture, rolling them into balls in the palms of your hands. Place these prepared meatballs on a baking sheet lined with kitchen parchment and allow them to cook in the hot oven for fifteen minutes before turning the pan around and cooking for an additional fifteen minutes.

6. Reduce the oven temperature to that of Fahrenheit four-hundred degrees.

7. Place the cooked meatballs in a large saucepan and add in the marinara sauce, heating it on a stove burner set to medium-low heat until the sauce is hot all the way through. Occasionally stir the chickpea meatballs in the marinara sauce so that they are evenly coated.

8. Fill the sub rolls with the meatballs and sauce, top them with the dairy-free cheese, and place them in the hot often on the baking sheet for fifteen minutes, or until the dairy-free cheese is melted and the bread is warm. Enjoy the subs hot and fresh from the oven.

Nutrition: Number of Calories in Individual **Servings:** 376 Protein Grams: 16 Fat Grams: 9 Total Carbohydrates Grams: 57 Net Carbohydrates Grams: 67

GRAINS AND BEANS

Black-Eyed Peas and Corn Salad

Preparation Time: 30 minutes

Cooking Time: 50 minutes

Servings: 4

Ingredients:

- 2½ cups cooked black-eyed peas

- 3 ears corn, kernels removed

- 1 medium ripe tomato, diced

- ½ medium red onion, peeled and diced small

- ½ red bell pepper, deseeded and diced small

- 1 jalapeño pepper, deseeded and minced

- ½ cup finely chopped cilantro

- ¼ cup plus 2 tablespoons balsamic vinegar

- 3 cloves garlic, peeled and minced

- 1 teaspoon toasted and ground cumin seeds

Directions:

1. Stir together all the ingredients in a large bowl and refrigerate for about 1 hour, or until well chilled.

2. Serve chilled.

Nutrition: Calories: 247 Fat: 1.8g Carbs: 47.6g Protein: 12.9g Fiber: 11.7g

Walnut, Coconut, and Oat Granola

Preparation Time: 15 minutes

Cooking Time: 1 hour 40 minutes

Servings: 4

Ingredients:

- 1 cup chopped walnuts

- 1 cup unsweetened, shredded coconut

- 2 cups rolled oats

- 1 teaspoon ground cinnamon

- 2 tablespoons hemp seeds

- 2 tablespoons ground flaxseeds

- 2 tablespoons chia seeds

- ¾ teaspoon salt (optional)

- ¼ cup maple syrup

- ¼ cup water

- 1 teaspoon vanilla extract

- ½ cup dried cranberries

Directions:

1. Preheat the oven to 250°F (120°C). Line a baking sheet with parchment paper.

2. Mix the walnuts, coconut, rolled oats, cinnamon, hemp seeds, flaxseeds, chia seeds, and salt (if desired) in a bowl.

3. Combine the maple syrup and water in a saucepan. Bring to a boil over medium heat, then pour in the bowl of walnut mixture.

4. Add the vanilla extract to the bowl of mixture. Stir to mix well. Pour the mixture in the baking sheet, then level with a spatula so the mixture coat the bottom evenly.

5. Place the baking sheet in the preheated oven and bake for 90 minutes or until browned and crispy. Stir the mixture every 15 minutes.

6. Remove the baking sheet from the oven. Allow to cool for 10 minutes, then serve with dried cranberries on top.

Nutrition: Calories: 1870 Fat: 115.8g Carbs: 238.0g Protein: 59.8g Fiber: 68.9g

Ritzy Fava Bean Ratatouille

Preparation Time: 15 minutes

Cooking Time: 40 minutes

Servings: 4

Ingredients:

- 1 medium red onion, peeled and thinly sliced

- 2 tablespoons low-sodium vegetable broth

- 1 large eggplant, stemmed and cut into ½-inch dice

- 1 red bell pepper, seeded and diced

- 2 cups cooked fava beans

- 2 Roma tomatoes, chopped

- 1 medium zucchini, diced

- 2 cloves garlic, peeled and finely chopped

- ¼ cup finely chopped basil

- Salt, to taste (optional)

- Ground black pepper, to taste

Directions:

1. Add the onion to a saucepan and sauté for 7 minutes or until caramelized.

2. Add the vegetable broth, eggplant and red bell pepper to the pan and sauté for 10 more minutes.

3. Add the fava beans, tomatoes, zucchini, and garlic to the pan and sauté for an additional 5 minutes.

4. Reduce the heat to medium-low. Put the pan lid on and cook for 15 minutes or until the vegetables are soft. Stir the vegetables halfway through.

5. Transfer them onto a large serving plate. Sprinkle with basil, salt (if desired), and black pepper before serving.

Nutrition: Calories: 114 Fat: 1.0g Carbs: 24.2g Protein: 7.4g Fiber: 10.3g

DRINK

Lemon Mousse

Preparation Time: 10 minutes

Cooking Time: 0 minute

Servings: 2

Ingredients:

- 14 oz. coconut milk
- 12 drops liquid stevia
- 1/2 tsp lemon extract
- 1/4 tsp turmeric

Directions:

1. Place coconut milk can in the refrigerator for overnight. Scoop out thick cream into a mixing bowl.

2. Add remaining ingredients to the bowl and whip using a hand mixer until smooth.

3. Transfer mousse mixture to a zip-lock bag and pipe into small serving glasses. Place in refrigerator.

4. Serve chilled and enjoy.

Nutrition: Calories: 189 Total Carbohydrate: 2 g Cholesterol: 13 mg Total Fat: 7 g Fiber: 2 g Protein: 15 g Sodium: 321 mg

Chocó Chia Pudding

Preparation Time: 10 minutes

Cooking Time: 0 minutes

Servings: 6

Ingredients:

- 2 1/2 cups coconut milk

- 2 scoops stevia extract powder

- 6 tbsp. cocoa powder

- 1/2 cup chia seeds

- 1/2 tsp vanilla extract

- 1/8 cup xylitol

- 1/8 tsp salt

Directions:

1. Add all ingredients into the blender and blend until smooth.

2. Pour mixture into the glass container and place in refrigerator.

3. Serve chilled and enjoy.

Nutrition: Calories: 178 Total Carbohydrate: 3 g Cholesterol: 3 mg Total Fat: 17 g Fiber: g Protein: 9 g Sodium: 297 mg

Spiced Buttermilk

Preparation Time: 5 minutes

Cooking Time: 0 minute

Servings: 2

Ingredients:

- 3/4 teaspoon ground cumin

- 1/4 teaspoon sea salt

- 1/8 teaspoon ground black pepper

- 2 mint leaves

- 1/8 teaspoon lemon juice

- ¼ cup cilantro leaves

- 1 cup of chilled water

- 1 cup vegan yogurt, unsweetened

- Ice as needed

Directions:

1. Place all the ingredients in the order in a food processor or blender, except for cilantro and ¼ teaspoon cumin, and then pulse for 2 to 3 minutes at high speed until smooth.

2. Pour the milk into glasses, top with cilantro and cumin, and then serve.

Nutrition: Calories: 211 Total Carbohydrate: 7 g Cholesterol: 13 mg Total Fat: 18 g Fiber: 3 g Protein: 17 g Sodium: 289 mg

Soothing Ginger Tea Drink

Preparation Time: 5 minutes

Cooking Time: 2 hours 20 minutes

Servings: 8

Ingredients:

- 1 tablespoon of minced gingerroot

- 2 tablespoons of honey

- 15 green tea bags

- 32 fluid ounce of white grape juice

- 2 quarts of boiling water

Directions:

1. Pour water into a 4-quarts slow cooker, immerse tea bags, cover the cooker and let stand for 10 minutes.

2. After 10 minutes, remove and discard tea bags and stir in remaining ingredients.

3. Return cover to slow cooker, then plug in and let cook at high heat setting for 2 hours or until heated through.

4. When done, strain the liquid and serve hot or cold.

Nutrition: Calories 232 Carbs: 7.9g Protein: 15.9g Fat: 15.1g

Nice Spiced Cherry Cider

Preparation Time: 1 hour 5 minutes

Cooking Time: 3 hours

Servings: 16

Ingredients:

- 2 cinnamon sticks, each about 3 inches long

- 6-ounce of cherry gelatin

- 4 quarts of apple cider

Directions:

1. Using a 6-quarts slow cooker, pour the apple cider and add the cinnamon stick.

2. Stir, then cover the slow cooker with its lid. Plug in the cooker and let it cook for 3 hours at the high heat setting or until it is heated thoroughly.

3. Then add and stir the gelatin properly, then continue cooking for another hour.

4. When done, remove the cinnamon sticks and serve the drink hot or cold.

Nutrition: Calories 78 Carbs: 13.2g Protein: 2.8g Fat: 1.5g

DESSERT

Peach-Mango Crumble (Pressure cooker)

Preparation Time: 10 minutes

Cooking Time: 6 minutes

Servings: 4-6

Ingredient:

- 3 cups chopped fresh or frozen peaches

- 3 cups chopped fresh or frozen mangos

- 4 tablespoons unrefined sugar or pure maple syrup, divided

- 1 cup gluten-free rolled oats

- ½ cup shredded coconut, sweetened or unsweetened

- 2 tablespoons coconut oil or vegan margarine

Directions:

1. Preparing the Ingredients. In a 6- to 7-inch round baking dish, toss together the peaches, mangos, and 2 tablespoons of sugar. In a food processor, combine the oats, coconut, coconut oil, and remaining 2

tablespoons of sugar. Pulse until combined. (If you use maple syrup, you'll need less coconut oil. Start with just the syrup and add oil if the mixture isn't sticking together.) Sprinkle the oat mixture over the fruit mixture.

2. Cover the dish with aluminum foil. Put a trivet in the bottom of your electric pressure cooker's cooking pot and pour in a cup or two of water. Using a foil sling or silicone helper handles, lower the pan onto the trivet.

3. High pressure for 6 minutes. Close and lock the lid, and select High Pressure for 6 minutes.

4. Pressure Release. Once the Cooking Time: is complete, quick release the pressure. Unlock and remove the lid.

5. Let cool for a few minutes before carefully lifting out the dish with oven mitts or tongs. Scoop out portions to serve.

Nutrition: Calories 275 Fat 19 g Carbohydrates 19 g Sugar 4 g Protein 14 g Cholesterol 60 mg

Almond-Date Energy Bites

Preparation Time: 5 minutes

Cooking Time: 15 minutes

Servings: 24

Ingredients:

- 1 cup dates, pitted

- 1 cup unsweetened shredded coconut

- ¼ cup chia seeds

- ¾ cup ground almonds

- ¼ cup cocoa nibs, or non-dairy chocolate chips

Directions:

1. Purée everything in a food processor until crumbly and sticking together, pushing down the sides whenever necessary to keep it blending. If you don't have a food processor, you can mash soft Medjool dates. But if you're using harder baking dates, you'll have to soak them and then try to purée them in a blender.

2. Form the mix into 24 balls and place them on a baking sheet lined with parchment or waxed paper. Put in the fridge to set for about 15 minutes. Use the softest dates you can find. Medjool dates are the best for this purpose. The hard dates you see in the baking aisle of your

supermarket are going to take a long time to blend up. If you use those, try soaking them in water for at least an hour before you start, and then draining.

Nutrition: Calories 171 Fat 4 g Carbohydrates 7 g Sugar 7 g Protein 22 g Cholesterol 65 mg

Pumpkin Pie Cups
(Pressure cooker)

Preparation Time: 5 minutes

Cooking Time: 6 minutes

Servings: 4-6

Ingredients:

- 1 cup canned pumpkin purée

- 1 cup nondairy milk

- 6 tablespoons unrefined sugar or pure maple syrup (less if using sweetened milk), plus more for sprinkling

- ¼ cup spelt flour or whole-grain flour

- ½ teaspoon pumpkin pie spice

- Pinch salt

Directions:

1. Preparing the Ingredients. In a medium bowl, stir together the pumpkin, milk, sugar, flour, pumpkin pie spice, and salt. Pour the mixture into 4 heat-proof ramekins. Sprinkle a bit more sugar on the top of each, if you like. Put a trivet in the bottom of your electric pressure cooker's cooking pot and pour in a cup or two of water. Place

the ramekins onto the trivet, stacking them if needed (3 on the bottom, 1 on top).

2. High pressure for 6 minutes. Close and lock the lid, and select High Pressure for 6 minutes.

3. Pressure Release. Once the Cooking Time: is complete, quick release the pressure. Unlock and remove the lid. Let cool for a few minutes before carefully lifting out the ramekins with oven mitts or tongs. Let cool for at least 10 minutes before serving.

Nutrition: Calories 152 Fat 4 g Carbohydrates 4 g Sugar 8 g Protein 18 g Cholesterol 51 mg

Fudgy Brownies (Pressure cooker)

Preparation Time: 10 minutes

Cooking Time: 5 minutes

Servings: 4-6

Ingredients:

- 3 ounces dairy-free dark chocolate
- 1 tablespoon coconut oil or vegan margarine
- ½ cup applesauce
- 2 tablespoons unrefined sugar
- 1/3 cup whole-grain flour
- ½ teaspoon baking powder
- Pinch salt

Directions:

1. Preparing the Ingredients. Put a trivet in your electric pressure cooker's cooking pot and pour in a cup or two of two of water. Select Sauté or Simmer. In a large heat-proof glass or ceramic bowl, combine the chocolate and coconut oil. Place the bowl over the top of your pressure cooker, as you would a double boiler. Stir occasionally until

the chocolate is melted, then turn off the pressure cooker. Stir the applesauce and sugar into the chocolate mixture. Add the flour, baking powder, and salt and stir just until combined. Pour the batter into 3 heat-proof ramekins. Put them in a heat-proof dish and cover with aluminum foil. Using a foil sling or silicone helper handles, lower the dish onto the trivet. (Alternately, cover each ramekin with foil and place them directly on the trivet, without the dish.)

2. High pressure for 6 minutes. Close and lock the lid, and select High Pressure for 5 minutes.

3. Pressure Release. Once the Cooking Time: is complete, quick release the pressure. Unlock and remove the lid.

4. Let cool for a few minutes before carefully lifting out the dish, or ramekins, with oven mitts or tongs. Let cool for a few minutes more before serving.

5. Top with fresh raspberries and an extra drizzle of melted chocolate.

Nutrition: Calories 256 Fat 29 g Carbohydrates 1 g Sugar 0.5 g Protein 11 g Cholesterol 84 mg

Chocolate Macaroons

Preparation Time: 10 minutes

Cooking Time: 15 minutes

Servings: 8

Ingredients:

- 1 cup unsweetened shredded coconut

- 2 tablespoons cocoa powder

- 2/3 cup coconut milk

- ¼ cup agave

- pinch of sea salt

Directions:

1. Preparing the Ingredients.

2. Preheat the oven to 350°F. Line a baking sheet with parchment paper. In a medium saucepan, cook all the ingredients over -medium-high heat until a firm dough is formed. Scoop the dough into balls and place on the baking sheet.

3. Bake for 15 minutes, remove from the oven, and let cool on the baking sheet.

4. Serve cooled macaroons or store in a tightly sealed container for up to

Nutrition: Calories 371 Fat 15 g Carbohydrates 7 g Sugar 2 g Protein 41 g Cholesterol 135 mg

Express Coconut Flax Pudding

Preparation Time: 5 minutes

Cooking Time: 15 minutes

Servings: 4

Ingredients:

- 1 Tbsp. coconut oil softened

- 1 Tbsp. coconut cream

- 2 cups coconut milk canned

- 3/4 cup ground flax seed

- 4 Tbsp. coconut palm sugar (or to taste)

Directions:

1. Press SAUTÉ button on your Instant Pot

2. Add coconut oil, coconut cream, coconut milk, and ground flaxseed.

3. Stir about 5 - 10 minutes.

4. Lock lid into place and set on the MANUAL setting for 5 minutes.

5. When the timer beeps, press "Cancel" and carefully flip the Quick Release valve to let the pressure out.

6. Add the palm sugar and stir well.

7. Taste and adjust sugar to taste.

8. Allow pudding to cool down completely.

9. Place the pudding in an airtight container and refrigerate for up to 2 weeks.

Nutrition: Calories: 140 Fat: 2g Fiber: 23g Carbs: 22g Protein: 47g

Full-flavored Vanilla Ice Cream

Preparation Time: 5 minutes

Cooking Time: 20 minutes

Servings: 8

Ingredients:

- 1 1/2 cups canned coconut milk

- 1 cup coconut whipping cream

- 1 frozen banana cut into chunks

- 1 cup vanilla sugar

- 3 Tbsp. apple sauce

- 2 tsp pure vanilla extract

- 1 tsp Xanthan gum or agar-agar thickening agent

Directions:

1. Add all ingredients in a food processor; process until all ingredients combined well.

2. Place the ice cream mixture in a freezer-safe container with a lid over.

3. Freeze for at least 4 hours.

4. Remove frozen mixture to a bowl and beat with a mixer to break up the ice crystals.

5. Repeat this process 3 to 4 times.

6. Let the ice cream at room temperature for 15 minutes before serving.

Nutrition: Calories: 342 Fat: 15g Fiber: 11g Carbs: 8gProtein: 10g

OTHER RECIPES

Crunchy Granola

Preparation Time: 10 Minutes

Cooking Time: 20 Minutes

Servings: 1

Ingredients:

- ½ cup Oats

- Dash of Salt

- 2 tbsp. Vegetable Oil

- 3 tbsp. Maple Syrup

- 1/3 cup Apple Cider Vinegar

- ½ cup Almonds

- 1 tsp. Cardamom, grounded

Directions:

1. Preheat the oven to 375 °F.

2. After that, mix oats, pistachios, salt, and cardamom in a large bowl.

3. Next, spoon in the vegetable oil and maple syrup to the mixture.

4. Then, transfer the mixture to a parchment-paper-lined baking sheet.

5. Bake them for 13 minutes or until the mixture is toasted. Tip: Check on them now and then. Spread it out well.

6. Return the sheet to the oven for further ten minutes.

7. From your oven remove the sheet and allow it to cool completely.

8. Serve and enjoy.

Nutrition: Calories: 763Kcal Proteins: 12.9g Carbohydrates: 64.8g Fat: 52.4g

Chickpea Scramble Bowl

Preparation Time: 10 Minutes

Cooking Time: 10 Minutes

Servings: Makes 2 Bowl

Ingredients:

- ¼ of 1 Onion, diced

- 15 oz. Chickpeas

- 2 Garlic cloves, minced

- ½ tsp. Turmeric

- ½ tsp. Black Pepper

- ½ tsp. Extra Virgin Olive Oil

- ½ tsp. Salt

Directions:

1. Begin by placing the chickpeas in a large bowl along with a bit of water.

2. Soak for few minutes and then mash the chickpeas lightly with a fork while leaving some of them in the whole form.

3. Next, spoon in the turmeric, pepper, and salt to the bowl. Mix well.

4. Then, heat oil in a medium-sized skillet over medium-high heat.

5. Once the oil becomes hot, stir in the onions.

6. Sauté the onions for 3 to 4 minutes or until softened.

7. Then, add the garlic and cook for further 1 minute or until aromatic.

8. After that, stir in the mashed chickpeas. Cook for another 4 minutes or until thickened.

9. Serve along with micro greens. Place the greens at the bottom, followed by the scramble, and top it with cilantro or parsley.

Nutrition: Calories: 801Kcal Proteins: 41.5g Carbohydrates: 131.6g Fat: 14.7g